First Step for Writing

Myeong-Hee Seong
Yoon-Hee Shin

BAEKSAN Publishing Co

Contents

Unit 1 About Me _8

1 Reading for Ideas 8
2 Focusing on Grammar 9
3 Learning Sentence Structures 12
4 Common Mistakes 13
5 Writing Practice I 14
6 Writing Practice II 16

Unit 2 My Friend _18

1 Reading for Ideas 18
2 Focusing on Grammar 19
3 Learning Sentence Structures 22
4 Common Mistakes 23
5 Writing Practice I 24
6 Writing Practice II 26

Unit 3 My Family — 28

1 Reading for Ideas ······ 28
2 Focusing on Grammar ······ 29
3 Learning Sentence Structures ······ 32
4 Common Mistakes ······ 33
5 Writing Practice I ······ 34
6 Writing Practice II ······ 36

Unit 4 My Day — 38

1 Reading for Ideas ······ 38
2 Focusing on Grammar ······ 39
3 Learning Sentence Structures ······ 42
4 Common Mistakes ······ 43
5 Writing Practice I ······ 44
6 Writing Practice II ······ 46

Unit 5 My Favorite Sports — 48

1 Reading for Ideas ······ 48
2 Focusing on Grammar ······ 49
3 Learning Sentence Structures ······ 52
4 Common Mistakes ······ 53
5 Writing Practice I ······ 54
6 Writing Practice II ······ 56

Unit 6 My Dream Job _58

1 Reading for Ideas 58
2 Focusing on Grammar 59
3 Learning Sentence Structures 62
4 Common Mistakes 63
5 Writing Practice 1 64
6 Writing Practice II 66

Unit 7 Letter _68

1 Reading for Ideas 68
2 Focusing on Grammar 69
3 Learning Sentence Structures 72
4 Common Mistakes 73
5 Writing Practice I 74
6 Writing Practice II 76

Unit 8 E-Mail _78

1 Reading for Ideas 78
2 Focusing on Grammar 79
3 Learning Sentence Structures 82
4 Common Mistakes 83
5 Writing Practice I 84
6 Writing Practice II 86

Unit 9 Having a Pet — 88

1 Reading for Ideas ········· 88
2 Focusing on Grammar ········· 89
3 Learning Sentence Structures ········· 92
4 Common Mistakes ········· 93
5 Writing Practice I ········· 94
6 Writing Practice II ········· 96

Unit 10 Shopping for Groceries — 98

1 Reading for Ideas ········· 98
2 Focusing on Grammar ········· 99
3 Learning Sentence Structures ········· 102
4 Common Mistakes ········· 103
5 Writing Practice I ········· 104
6 Writing Practice II ········· 106

Unit 11 Invitation — 108

1 Reading for Ideas ········· 108
2 Focusing on Grammar ········· 109
3 Learning Sentence Structures ········· 112
4 Common Mistakes ········· 113
5 Writing Practice I ········· 114
6 Writing Practice II ········· 116

Unit 12 Poster — 118

1 Reading for Ideas 118
2 Focusing on Grammar 119
3 Learning Sentence Structures 122
4 Common Mistakes 123
5 Writing Practice I 124
6 Writing Practice II 126

Answer Key — 129

References — 166

UNIT 1

About Me

1 Reading for Ideas

Read 'About Me' and then answer the questions.

About Me

My name is Mary. I am a girl from Malaysia. I'm the only girl in a family of four children. I have three younger brothers. They are troublesome, but I love them a lot. I am a sophomore at a university in New York. I am studying linguistics and English literature. I want to be an English teacher after graduating. I am not tall and a little bit overweight. I have short curly black hair with small black eyes.

I like reading, especially sci-fi novels. I have a big collection of novels of all kinds! I am also a music lover. I spend most of my afternoons listening to music.

1. Where does she come from?

2. What's she majoring in?

3. What does she like to do?

4. What does she look like?

5. What do you like to do in your free time?

2 Focusing on Grammar

Look at the examples below and then make the sentences similar to the examples.

1. want(would like) + 목적어(명사)
   ➡ '명사'를 원하다

- I want(would like) a sandwich and milk for my breakfast.
- He wants(would like) something to eat.

I ______________________________.

She ______________________________.

2. want(would like) + 목적어(to부정사)
   ➡ 'to부정사' 하고 싶다, 'to부정사' 하기를 원하다

- The government wants(would like) to implement a job sharing policy.
- She wants(would like) to go there with her sister.

I ______________________________.

He ______________________________.

3. want(would like) + 목적어(명사) + 목적보어(to부정사)
   ➡ '명사'가 'to부정사' 하기를 원한다

- I want(would like) you to eat an apple.
- He wants(would like) himself to be reported to the police.

I ____.

She ____.

4. want(would like) + 목적어(명사) + 목적보어(과거분사)
   ➡ '명사'가 '과거분사' 되기를 원하다

- She wanted(would like) the letter rewritten once again.
- We want(would like) the watch repaired right now.

I ____.

They ____.

5. like + 목적어(명사)
   ➡ '명사'를 좋아하다

- I like oranges.
- My mother likes green tea.

I ____.

She ____.

6. like + 목적어(to부정사 / 동명사)
   ➡ 'to부정사 / 동명사' 하기를 좋아하다

- I like to go shopping with my friend.
- My sister likes going shopping with her friend.

I ____.

She ____.

7. spend + 시간 / 돈 + 동명사
➡ '동명사' 하는데 시간 / 돈을 사용하다

- I spent three hours repairing the clock.
- She spent $1000 buying her clothes a few days ago.

I ____.

He ____.

8. spend + 시간 / 돈 + on + 명사
➡ '명사'에 시간 / 돈을 쓰다

- I spend a lot of money on books.
- Nowadays many people spend too much money and time on healthcare.

I ____.

He ____.

3 Learning Sentence Structures

Write the sentences in English using the words in the parentheses.

1. 그는 일본 도쿄에 살고 있다. (Tokyo, Japan)

2. 나는 책을 읽으면서 음악을 듣는 것을 좋아한다. (listen to)

3. Mary는 대학 졸업 후 은행원이 되고 싶어한다. (after graduating)

4. 우리 학교의 영어선생님은 40대이다. (in his 40s)

5. 그의 엄마는 앞으로 그가 선생님이 되기를 원한다. (to be a teacher)

6. 한국의 부모님들은 사교육에 많은 돈을 소비한다. (private education)

7. 한국인들은 영어 공부하는데 너무 많은 돈과 시간을 소비한다.

8. 그녀는 혼자 밤에 컴퓨터게임 하는 것을 좋아한다. (play computer games)

4 Common Mistakes

Correct the twelve mistakes and then rewrite the paragraph.

my name is Lee, Soonhee. I am from Korea. I am majoring at chilc development at an university in the U.S. I am a university junior. after graduating, i want to teach kids at a kindergarten in Korea. I lives with my sister's family here. I am a short and slim. Also, I have short curly hair with big black eye. I am a kind of introverted person. I like to staying home and read comic books. I like my classmates. They is very kind and friendly.

5 Writing Practice I

Look at the mind map and then answer the questions.

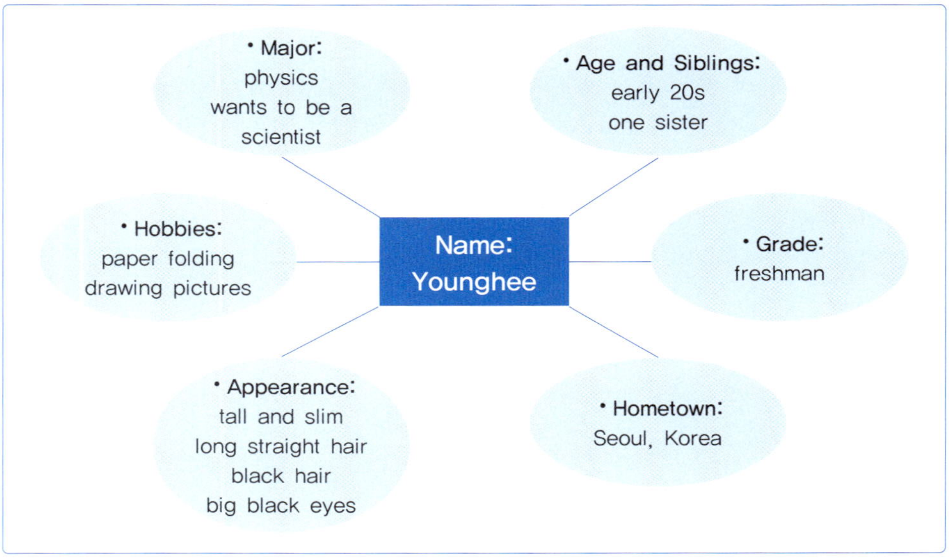

1. What's the girl's name?

2. How old is she?

3. How many sisters or brothers does she have?

4. What is she studying and why?

5. What does she like to do in her free time?

Write about Younghee using the mind map.

6 Writing Practice II

Fill in the mind map by writing information about yourself in the boxes below.

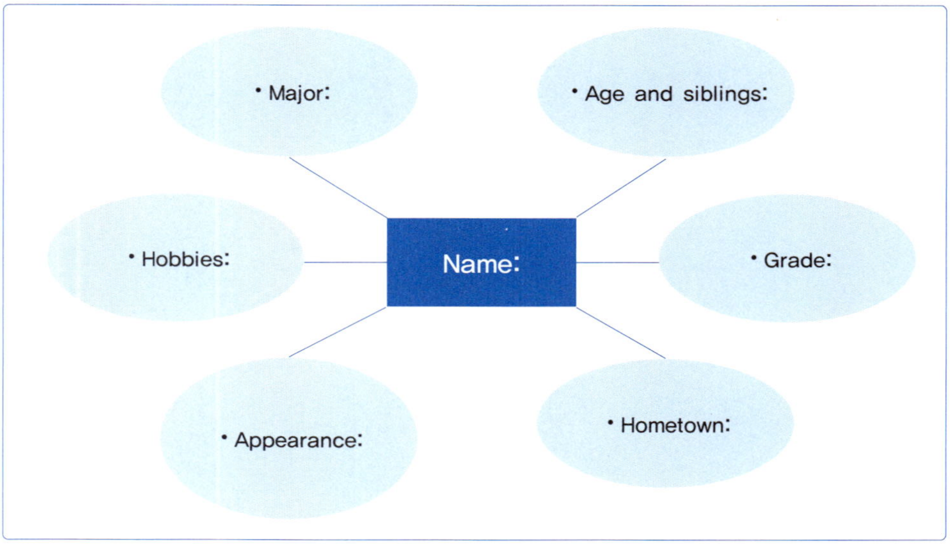

Write about yourself using the information you wrote in the mind map.

UNIT

2 My Friend

1 Reading for Ideas

Read 'My Friend' and then answer the questions.

My Friend

This is my best friend Pablo from Spain. He is 22 years old, and he is a junior at Madrid University. He is not tall, but he is not short either. He has a medium build. He has short blond hair with big blue eyes. He and I go to the same university. He is studying statistics, but I am studying mathematics. We study together and play soccer together. We sometimes go to movies and eat out together after class. He is a vegan. He does not eat animal byproducts such as eggs, milk, and butter. Like most vegans, he loves animals. He is energetic and outgoing, so he has lots of friends, including me. He always smiles and likes to help people. He likes taking pictures, and he is very good at it. I hope he and I will be best friends forever!

1. Who is Pablo?

2. What is he like?

3. What does he look like?

4. What's his major?

5. What does he like doing?

2 Focusing on Grammar

Look at the examples below and then make the sentences similar to the examples.

1. too
   ➡ 역시('긍정'과 함께)

- She is aloof, cold, and inaccessible, too.
- He is young, clever, and rich, too.
- Bill is ready, and I am too.

____.

____.

2. either
   ➡ 역시('부정'과 함께)

- I didn't read the book, either.
- I don't like eggs and meat, either.
- If you don't go, I won't go either.

____.

____.

3. be good at + 명사 / 동명사
   ➡ '명사 / 동명사'를 잘하다

- He is good at English.

- I am good at playing the piano.

____.

____.

4. be poor at + 명사 / 동명사
   ➡ '명사 / 동명사'를 잘못하다

- My mom is poor at cooking.
- He is poor at mathematics.

____.

____.

5. play + 운동경기
   ➡ 운동경기를 하다

- He plays soccer with his classmates after school once a week.
- I play tennis with my friend every day for my health.

____.

____.

6. play + 관사 + 악기
   ➡ 악기를 다루다

- I started to play the piano at the age of 8.
- My brother practices playing the violin very hard for the competition.

____.

____.

7. 빈도부사 : always, often, sometimes, seldom, rarely, never
   ➡ be동사 뒤, 조동사 뒤, 일반동사 앞

- He is always late for school.
- I don't often get up early on Saturdays and Sundays.
- They sometimes eat out because they don't like cooking.
- She seldom skips her breakfast although she gets up late.

____.

____.

____.

____.

3 Learning Sentence Structures

Write the sentences in English using the words in the parentheses.

1. 그는 사과도 좋아하고 오렌지도 역시 좋아한다. (too)

2. 요즈음 나는 좀처럼 학교에 결석하지 않는다. (seldom)

3. 내 동생은 일찍 일어나지도 않고 학교에 일찍 가지도 않는다. (either)

4. 우리 아빠는 종종 친구와 직장이 끝난 후 테니스를 한다. (after work)

5. 내 친구는 부모님에게 항상 매우 친절하고 공손하다. (be polite to)

6. 우리 오빠는 수학은 잘하지만 영어는 못한다. (good, poor)

7. 내 친구와 나는 음악시간에 종종 바이올린을 함께 연주한다.

8. 나는 일요일에 때때로 여자친구와 영화를 보러 간다. (go to the movies)

4 Common Mistakes

Correct the fifteen mistakes and then rewrite the paragraph.

Let me introduce my friend to you. His name is Youngjae. He is at his early 20s. he is sophomore in Eulji University at Seongnam. He live in near Seongnam. He is not talls, but he is handsome. He has shortly straight black hairs with black eye. He is brave but humorous. He like read comic books. He always tell jokes to his friends, so he has many friend around his.

5 Writing Practice I

Look at the mind map about Amon's friend and then answer the questions.

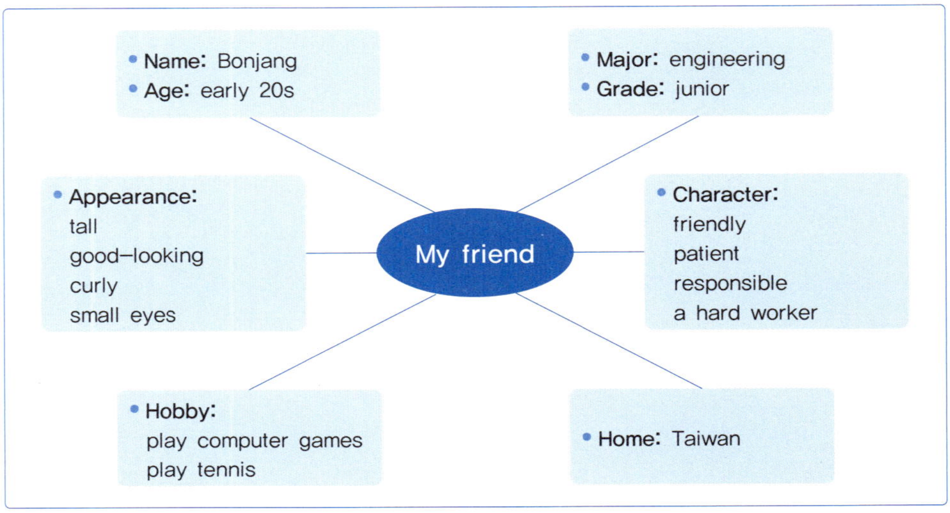

1. What's the name of Amon's friend?

2. What is he majoring in at the university?

3. What does he look like?

4. What kind of person is he?

5. What does he like to do in his free time?

Write about Amon's friend based upon the mind map.

6 Writing Practice II

Fill in the mind map by writing information about one of your friends in the boxes below.

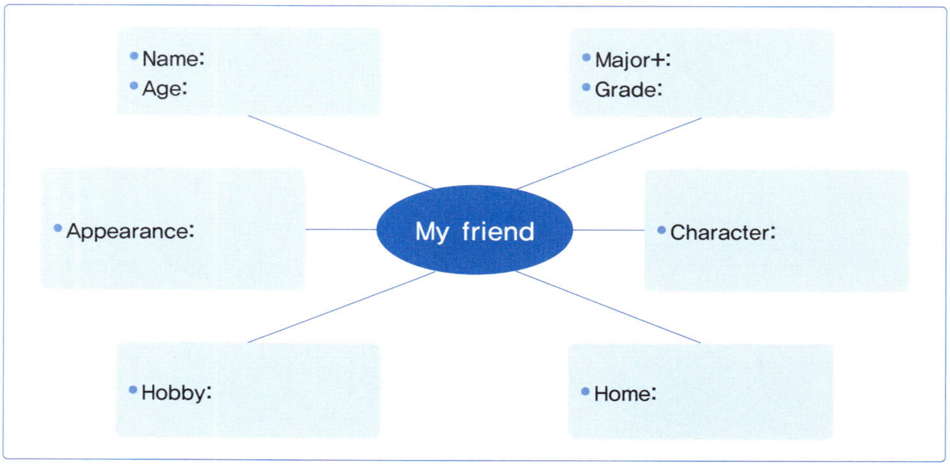

Write about your friend using the information you wrote in the mind map.

UNIT 3

My Family

1 Reading for Ideas

Read 'My Family' by Suzan and then answer the questions.

My Family

There are four people in my family – my father, mother, sister and me. My father is friendly, handsome and tall. He is a teacher at the high school my sister goes to. He comes home early and helps my sister with her homework. He likes cooking at home and sometimes cooks for us. My mother is beautiful and smart. She is short. Unlike my father, she does not like cooking. She runs a floral shop and likes taking care of flowers. My sister Wendy is 17 years old. She is a sophomore in high school. Her school is just about a 30 minute walk from home. My father and my sister usually go to school together. They prefer walking rather than taking a bus. She likes mathematics, but she does not like P.E. Our family does lots of fun things together everyday.

1. How many people are there in Suzan's family?

2. What does her father do?

3. What does her father like to do?

4. What does her mother look like?

5. What is her sister's favorite subject?

2 Focusing on Grammar

Look at the examples below and then make the sentences similar to the examples.

1. There is + 단수 주어(명사)
   ➡ '명사' 들이 있다

- There is an apple in the basket.
- There is no money in my pocket.

____.

____.

2. There are + 복수 주어(명사)
   ➡ '명사' 들이 있다

- There are over 2,000 small and medium sized medical centers in Gangnam.
- There are only nine countries that have succeeded in launching a space rocket.

____.

____.

3. How much + 명사(셀 수 없는) + is there?
   ➡ 얼마나 많은 '명사'들이 있습니까?

- How much water is there in the bottle?

➡ There is a little water in the bottle.

____?

➡ ____.

4. How many + 명사(셀 수 있는) + are there?
   ➡ 얼마나 많은 '명사'들이 있습니까?

- How many people are there in your family?
  ➡ There are four in my family.

____?

➡ ____.

5. a 10 minute walk : 도보로 10분　　a 15 minute break : 15분간 휴식
   a 5 page paper : 5페이지 리포트　　a 25 year old man : 25세 남자
   a 3 year jail sentence : 3년 감옥형
   a 20 day inspection : 20일 동안 검열

- It is a 10 minute walk to work from home.
- The judge handed down a 3 year jail sentence.

____.

____.

6. It takes + 사람 + 시간 + to부정사 = It takes + 시간 + for 사람 + to부정사
   ➡ '사람'이 'to부정사' 하는데 '시간'이 걸린다

- It took me 2 hours to finish my project.
- It may take 9 hours to get from Seoul to Busan, longer than last year.

____.

____.

7. How long does it take + 사람 + to부정사
   ➡ '사람' 이 'to부정사' 하는데 얼마나 시간이 걸리나?

- How long does it take you to finish your homework usually?
  ➡ Usually, it takes me 3 hours to finish my homework.
- How long will it take him to do it?
  ➡ It will take him 4 hours to do it.

____?

➡ ____.

____?

➡ ____.

8. help + 사람 + with + 명사 / 동명사
   ➡ '사람'이 '명사 / 동명사' 하는 것을 돕다

- Mary helped her sister with the work in the kitchen.
- Can you help me with this project please?

____.

3 Learning Sentence Structures

Write the sentences in English using the words in the parentheses.

1. 하루에 커피를 몇 잔 마십니까? (How much coffee ~)

2. 너는 너의 방을 청소하는데 얼마나 걸리니? (How long ~)

3. 그의 방 가운데에 소파와 의자가 있습니다. (There are)

4. 밖에 나가서 십분 동안 휴식을 합시다. (a 10 minute break)

5. 그는 매주 일요일 엄마가 세탁하는 것을 돕습니다. (the laundry)

6. 뇌물을 받아서 그는 10년형을 받았다. (take bribes, a 10 year jail term)

7. 빨간색을 선호하십니까? 오렌지색을 선호하십니까? (prefer)

8. 내 가방에는 책도 공책도 없습니다. (in my backpack)

4 Common Mistakes

Correct the fifteen mistakes and then rewrite the paragraph.

Here is Roberto's family's photo. there is four member in the family. their names are Mr. and Mrs. Baroni, Bruno and Roberto. Mr. Baroni is sit on the bed. A night table is beside the bed and window is between a dresser and a night table. There are a rug on the floor. Mr. Baroni work in the factory. Mrs. Baroni work in a office and always use a computer. Bruno play the violin with a bow. roberto likes to play the baseball. When he plays baseball, he wears a helmet and an uniform. He is a good pitcher.

5 Writing Practice I

Look at the idea map and then answer the questions.

Smith's Family

- **Father:**
  kind & smart
  likes to write interesting stories
  likes to tell stories
  a writer

- **Mother:**
  slim and shy
  likes to cook
  likes to take care of a garden
  a chef

- **Me:**
  cheerful and healthy

- **Sister:**
  pretty & cute
  18 years old
  goes to a high school

1. How many people are there in Smith's family?

2. What does Smith's mother like to do?

3. Where does his sister go?

4. What does Smith's father do?

Write about Smith's family using the mind map.

6 Writing Practice II

Fill in the mind map by writing information about your family in the boxes below.

MY Family

- Father:
- Mother:
- Me:
- Sister or Brother:

Write about your own family using the information you wrote in the mind map.

UNIT 4

My Day

1 Reading for Ideas

Read 'My Day' by Elias and then answer the questions.

My Day

I got up at 7:00 this morning. Because I didn't want to be late for school, I took a shower and got dressed quickly. I ate a sandwich for breakfast, brushed my teeth, and put on some makeup. At 8:00 I took the subway, and arrived at school at 8:40. My first class was English. I learned about writing. I wrote a funny story and told it to my classmates. All my classmates enjoyed my story and laughed a lot. I came back home around 4:00 p.m. At 6:00 p.m., I went to work. I work at the convenience store from 6:00 p.m. to 10:00 p.m. three times a week: Monday, Wednesday, and Friday. Around 10:00 p.m., I came back home from work. I did my homework and prepared for the next day's classes. It was an exhausting day.

1. What did Elias do after he got up?

2. How did she get to school?

3. What did she do in her first class?

4. What did she do after school?

5. When did she come back from work?

2 Focusing on Grammar

Look at the examples below and then make the sentences similar to the examples.

1. Because 주어 + 동사, 주어 + 동사 = 주어 + 동사 because 주어 + 동사
   ➡ ~때문에 ~하다

- Because I was hungry, I ate quickly.
- Presidential candidates try to woo overseas voters because these ballots could be a major factor in the final result.

____.

____.

2. because of(due to) 명사 / 동명사
   ➡ ~때문에

- Due to power failure, the concert was postponed.
- We changed our plans because of rain.
- About half of the smokers in the world will die because of smoking.

____.

____.

3. tell + 간접목적어(사람) + 직접목적어(사물)
   = tell + 직접목적어(사물) + to 간접목적어(사람)
   ➡ '사람'에게 '사물'을 말해주다

- He told me the story when I met him yesterday.
- I sometimes tell my classmates (about) my experiences in Africa.

______________________________.

______________________________.

4. once a week / twice a week / three times a week
   ➡ 일주일에 한 번, 두 번, 세 번

- My sister works at the restaurant twice a week.
- I have heard the song 'Gangnam style' many times.
- My mother goes shopping once a month.

______________________________.

______________________________.

______________________________.

5. at + 명사(시간)
   ➡ 시간의 전치사 'at'

- I usually get up at 7:00, but my sister gets up at 6:30.
- The class begins at 10:00 and ends at 12:00.

______________________________.

______________________________.

6. at + 명사(장소)
➡ 장소의 전치사 'at'

- I'll be at work until 5:30, but I'll be at home all evening.
- Were there many people at the party?

______________________________.

______________________________.

7. from 명사 to 명사
➡ ~부터 ~까지

- He and I traveled from Seoul to New York.
- Things are going from bad to worse.
- We stayed there from May to July last year.

______________________________.

______________________________.

3 Learning Sentence Structures

Write the sentences in English using the words in the parentheses.

1. 나는 매일 5시부터 8시까지 도서관에서 일한다. (from ~ to)

2. 그는 자주 모든 사람에게 재미있는 이야기를 한다. (funny stories)

3. 그녀는 어젯밤에 10시경에 잠자리에 들었다. (go to bed)

4. 나는 밤에 음악을 듣고 책을 읽는다. (at night)

5. 그는 술을 너무 많이 마셔서 똑바로 걸을 수가 없었다.
   (drink alcohol, walk straight)

6. 허리가 아파서 병원에 갔다. (backache)

7. 우리 부서는 한 달에 2번 회의를 한다. (twice a month)

8. 그는 어젯밤 9시에 나에게 전화했다. (last night)

4 Common Mistakes

Correct the eighteen mistakes and then rewrite the paragraph.

I got up this morning at 8:00. I was late, so I quickly wash my face. I drink a glass of milk and brush my teeth. And then, I feed my pet. I take a bus and arrived at school at 8:50 a.m. It takes about 30 minutes to get to school by bus. My first class was japanese. I learn about the Japanese alphabet. I did a good job in class and enjoy it After class I meet one of my friend and go to see a movie. Around 10:00 p.m. I come back home. My mother is little angry because I am late. I was so tire, but I do my homework.

5 Writing Practice I

Look at the mind map and then answer the questions.

John's Day

- **Before School**
  - get up at 6:30
  - take a shower
  - comb my hair
  - get dressed
  - eat breakfast
  - brush my teeth
  - feed my pet
- **At School**
  - arrive at school
  - take a test
  - have lunch with
- **After School**
  - go to the library
  - prepare for exams
  - go home at 8 p.m.
  - help my mom
  - do my homework
  - pack my backpack
  - go to bed at midnight

1. What did John do at 6:30?

2. What did John do at school?

3. What did John do at 8 p.m?

4. What did John do at the library?

5. When did John go to bed?

Write about John's day based on the mind map.

6 Writing Practice II

Fill in the mind map by writing information about your day in the boxes below.

My Day

- Before School
- At School
- After School

Write about your day using the information you wrote in the mind map.

UNIT 5

My Favorite Sports

1 Reading for Ideas

Read 'Playing Tennis' by Anderson and then answer the questions.

Playing Tennis

I like to play tennis because it helps me to be healthy. I'm not good at playing tennis, but I just enjoy it. Fall is a good season to play tennis because it is not so hot and not so cold. I play tennis with my friends once a week. I learned how to play tennis from my uncle two years ago. It was not easy. I wanted to play tennis well and practiced a lot at that time. I think practice is the best way to learn something. I am hoping that I can get a tennis scholarship to help pay for college. These days I am teaching it to my brother. I hope my brother can play it very well soon.

1. What sport does Anderson like to play?
2. What season is good for the sport? Why?
3. Who taught him how to play tennis?
4. What do you think is the best way to learn something?
5. What is he doing these days?

2 Focusing on Grammar

Look at the examples below and then make the sentences similar to the examples.

1. 비인칭 주어 'It'
   ➡ 거리, 명암, 계절, 기후, 시간

- How far is it to school from home?
  ➡ It is two miles from home.
- It is about a 10 minute walk to the station.

____.

____.

- It is mid-spring now.
- It is mid-autumn now.

____.

____.

- It is getting dark. Let's hurry.
- It gets dark early in the winter.

____.

____.

- Look at the clouds in the sky. It looks like snow.
- It was very hot and humid this summer.

____.

____.

- It has been 5 years since I got married.
- What time is it now?
  ➡ It is 3 o'clock.

____.

____.

2. enjoy + 목적어(명사)
   ➡ '명사'를 즐기다

- Did you enjoy your vacation?
- Please enjoy your meal.

____.

____.

3. enjoy + 목적어(동명사)
   ➡ '동명사'하는 것을 즐기다

- When I have time, I enjoy reading books.
- He enjoys talking to strangers about his old days.

____.

____.

4. I think that 주어+동사
   ➡ 'that' 이하라고 생각하다

- I think that it will rain tomorrow.
- My father thought that my sister told a lie two days ago.

____.

____.

5. I hope that 주어+동사
   ➡ 'that' 이하를 바라다, 기대하다

- My mother hopes that her son will pass the bar exam next year.
- I hope that the third time will be the charm.

____.

____.

6. hope+to부정사
   ➡ 'to부정사'를 바라다

- I hope to hear from you soon.
- This year, John hopes to visit more foreign countries than any of his friends.

____.

____.

3 Learning Sentence Structures

Write the sentences in English using the words in the parentheses.

1. 그는 내년에 승진하길 바란다. (get promoted)

2. 이맘때 치고는 따뜻하다. (for this time of the year)

3. 그는 키도 크고 똑똑하며 잘 생겼다고 생각한다. (intelligent)

4. 어제는 일요일이었다. (Sunday)

5. 그것이 완전히 거짓이라고 생각하지 않는다. (false)

6. 여기서 우체국까지는 얼마나 걸릴까요? (the post office)

7. 해외에 가면 나와 어머니는 쇼핑을 즐긴다. (go abroad)

8. 그는 그의 아버지 건강이 곧 회복되길 바란다. (get well soon)

4 Common Mistakes

Correct the fourteen mistakes and then rewrite the paragraph.

I likes skiing. Winter is good season for skiing. I learned how to skiing from my brother-in-law five year ago. It was hard to learning how to slide down the hill. I fell down many time in the snow, I didn't give up. I practice it very hard for a while. Now I enjoy skiing. It is cool. It is excite and thrilling, too. I need ski boot, ski poles, goggles, ski gloves for skiing. Also I need ski suit for it. I like it because it help me to be healthy. I hope winter come soon.

5 Writing Practice I

Look at the mind map and then answer the questions.

Badminton

- **When:** spring
- **Who you learned it from:** my father
- **Why you like it:** not hard, fun
- **What you need:** a racket, a shuttlecock
- **What you like to do:** pass the shuttlecock over the net
  hit the shuttlecock strongly
- **What you hope:** to be a good player

1. What sport do you like to play?

2. What season is good for the sport?

3. Who taught you how to play badminton?

4. What equipment do you need to play badminton?

5. What are you hoping for in the future?

Write an essay about Badminton based on the mind map.

6 Writing Practice II

Fill in the mind map by writing information about a sport you enjoy in the boxes below.

____

- When:
- Who you learned it from:
- Why you like it:
- What you need:
- What you like to do:
- What you hope:

Write about a sport you enjoy using the information you wrote in the mind map.

UNIT 6 My Dream Job

1 Reading for Ideas

Read 'My Dream Job' by Paul and then answer the questions.

My Dream Job

There are a lot of jobs in the world. It is difficult to choose one, but I want to be a chef after I graduate. When I was younger, my mom ran a small restaurant in our village. She was a wonderful chef and my neighbors enjoyed her cooking. At home, she made us lots of wonderful food such as veggie omelets and pancakes drizzled with maple syrup. She sometimes baked delicious cookies and bread for us. I was so happy when I helped my mom cook. It really made me want to be a chef so that I could make people happy. It is hard work to become a chef, but I know if I put my mind to it, I can do it.

1. What does Paul want to be?

2. Who is Paul's role model?

3. What did his mom do at home?

4. How did he feel when he helped his mom cook?

5. What should he do to be a chef?

2 Focusing on Grammar

Look at the examples below and then make the sentences similar to the examples.

1. make + 목적어(명사)
   ➡ '명사'를 만들다

- My mother made a dress for me.
- My father makes a variety of jackets to export to other countries.

____.

____.

2. make + 간접목적어(사람) + 직접목적어(사물)
   ➡ '사람'에게 '사물'을 만들어 주다

- My mother made me a dress.
- My mother made my friends delicious food.

____.

____.

3. make + 목적어(명사) + 목적보어(원형부정사)
   ➡ '명사'가 '원형부정사' 하게 하다

- Our teachers in school made us work very hard.
- He told everybody funny stories and made them laugh.

4. make + 목적어(명사) + 목적보어(과거분사)
➡ '명사'가 '과거분사'되게 하다

- Because I didn't speak English fluently, I had a hard time making myself understood in English.
- I made my hair cut.

5. help + 목적어(명사) + 목적보어(to부정사 / 원형부정사)
➡ '명사'가 'to부정사 / 원형부정사' 하도록 돕다

- Reading English newspapers everyday helps me learn (to learn) English.
- Nuts help me reduce (to reduce) the cholesterol level in my body.

6. so that 주어 + 동사
➡ '주어'가 '동사'하기 위하여, ~하도록, 그래서

- He tied them up so that they couldn't escape.
- We drank as little as possible so that we wouldn't run out of water.

____.

____.

7. so as to + 동사
   ➡ '동사'하기 위하여

- The stores would bring the price down in the last half-hour so as to get rid of everything before they closed.

____.

8. so ~ that 주어 + 동사
   ➡ 너무 ~해서 '주어'가 '동사' 하다

- She is so young that she can't do it by herself.

____.

9. so ~ as to + 동사
   ➡ 너무 ~해서 '주어'가 '동사' 하다

- His symptom was so unusual as to perplex even the specialist.

____.

3 Learning Sentence Structures

Write the sentences in English using the words in the parentheses.

1. 이 책은 내가 영문법을 공부하는데 도움이 될 것이다. (English grammar)

2. 그가 들어올 수 있도록 그에게 열쇠를 주었다. (come in)

3. 슬픈 소식이 나를 울렸다. (The sad news)

4. 이리 와서 설거지 좀 도와주세요. (wash the dishes)

5. 어제 오후에 나는 내 동생에게 연을 만들어주었다. (a kite)

6. 우리는 같은 문제를 반복하지 않기 위해서 협력해야 한다. (cooperate)

7. 지난 일요일 아빠가 우리를 위해서 빵과 과자를 만들었다. (bread)

8. 햇볕이 강해서 얼굴에 선크림을 발랐다. (wear sunscreen)

4 Common Mistakes

Correct the thirteen mistakes and then rewrite the paragraph.

I am interested in make people beautiful. After graduating, i want to be a hairdresser likely Ms. Lee at my town. She run many shops around the country. She is friend, pretty, and smart. There is a lot of customers in her shop all the time. Three year ago I met and told to her that I wanted to be a hairdresser somedays. She encouraged me and told me many things about be a hair dresser. I know that it isn't an easy to be a hair dresser like her. I should to try to practice more, and I will.

5 Writing Practice 1

Look at the mind map and then answer the questions.

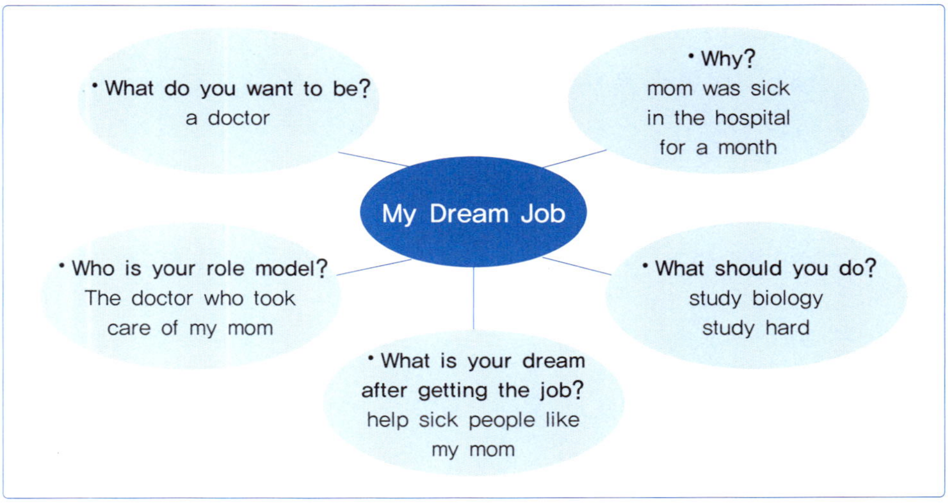

1. What do you want to do after graduating?

2. Why did you want to be a doctor?

3. What should you do to be a doctor?

4. What will you do as a doctor?

5. Who is your role model?

Write a paragraph based on the mind map.

6 Writing Practice II

Fill in the mind map by writing information about your dream job in the boxes below.

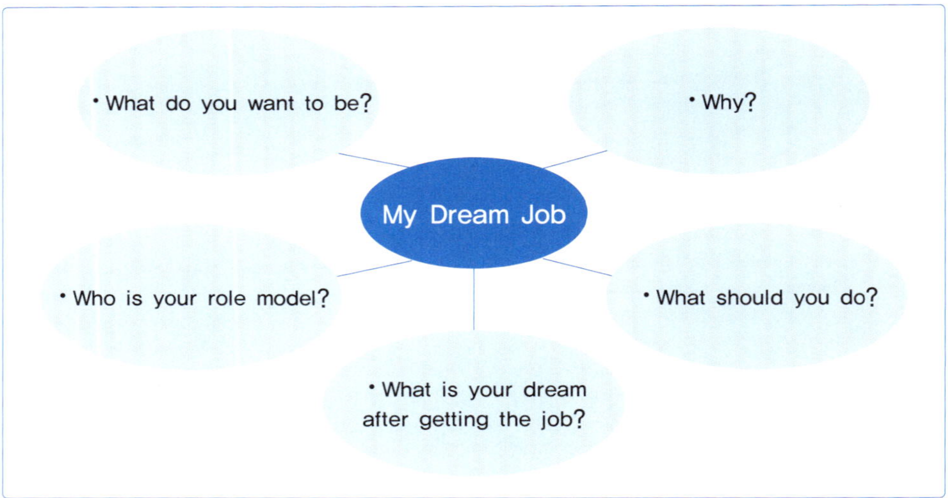

Write about your dream job using the information you wrote in the mind map.

UNIT 7

Letter

1 Reading for Ideas

Read Mary's letter and then answer the questions.

Wednesday, November 15th

Dear Wendy,

How are you doing? I'm doing well.

Thanks for the letter about your favorite subject. In your last letter, you said you like biology the most in your last letter, but it is my third favorite subject. My favorite subject is English and my second favorite is chemistry. I can learn how to write an essay in English class. Tomorrow I have English class. I need to bring an English-Spanish dictionary to class. I often look up words in the dictionary to write my essay during class. Now, I am thinking of what I will write about tomorrow. I'm very excited about this class. Please tell me about your school life!

Take care!

Sincerely,
Mary

1. Who wrote the letter?
2. Who did Mary write it to?
3. What class does Mary like the most? How about Wendy?
4. What should Mary bring to class tomorrow?
5. What will Mary do during English class tomorrow?

2 Focusing on Grammar

Look at the examples below and then make the sentences similar to the examples.

1. 의문사(what, where, how, when) + to부정사
   ➡ 무엇을, 어디로, 어떻게, 언제 'to부정사' 해야 할지

- I was so surprised that I didn't know what to do.
- After reviewing the projects, I'll decide what to continue and what to scrape.

____.

____.

2. during + 명사(언제) / for + 명사(기간)
   ➡ ~ 동안에

- The university will ban alcohol sales during festivals.
- I lived in America for 5 years.

____.

____.

3. While 주어 + 동사, 주어 + 동사 = 주어 + 동사 while 주어 + 동사
   ➡ ~ 동안에 ~하다

- I heard the news while I was driving.
- While you were away, there was a fire in town.

____.

____.

4. need + 목적어(명사)
➡ '명사'가 필요하다

- Do you need any help?
- I need a ruler and a compass for the class.

____.

____.

5. need + 목적어(to부정사)
➡ 'to부정사'할 필요가 있다

- We need to accept and understand cultures of other countries.
- She needs to put in more time in developing her skills.

____.

____.

6. need + 목적어(동명사)
➡ '동명사'될 필요가 있다

- The battery in the cell phone needs changing.
- The chapter in this grammar book needs rewriting.

____.

____.

7. need + 목적어(명사) + 목적보어(to부정사)
➡ '명사'가 'to부정사'해 주었으면 좋겠다

- I need him to rewrite the paper.
- I need my husband to help with the house chores.

____.

____.

8. 감정분사(bored / boring, excited / exciting, surprised / surprising)
➡ 사람이 주어일 때 : '과거분사'가 보어 역할
사물이 주어일 때 : '현재분사'가 보어 역할

- Jane is bored because her job is boring.
- I'm not interested in my job anymore.
- The game is exciting so I am excited.

____.

____.

____.

3 Learning Sentence Structures

Write the sentences in English using the words in the parentheses.

1. 당황해서 어떻게 해야 할지 몰랐다. (at a loss)

2. 모든 사람이 그가 시험에 합격해서 놀랐다. (pass)

3. 나는 그녀가 그 과제를 빨리 끝내주었으면 좋겠다. (the project)

4. 영화가 실망스러워서 우리는 실망했다. (disappoint)

5. 나는 지난 주말에 5시간 동안 영어공부를 했다. (last weekend)

6. 지난 겨울방학에 영어공부하러 미국에 갔었다. (last winter vacation)

7. 그는 책을 읽는 동안에 재미있는 무언가를 배웠다. (something interesting)

8. 수업 중에 친구로부터 문자를 받았다. (text message)

4 Common Mistakes

Correct the sixteen mistakes and then rewrite the paragraph.

May 10th, Monday

Dear Jeongsuk,

How have you been do? I am fine. It is really sunny day tocay. All kinds of flowers is blooming. I'm sitting in the grass. There is many students around I. Some are talking with their friends and other are reading and relaxing. It is a beautiful scene, isn't it? I'm happy to hearing that you are coming to California visiting me. It's not too hot and not too cold, too. I have five class: composition, grammar, vocabulary, speaking, and reading every weeks. I have three classes a day and study twenty-four hour a week. After class, I enjoy to talk with my classmates from other country. They are mostly from Asia. I hope I can meet you as soon as possible.

Take care

Sincerely,

Yoon

5 Writing Practice I

Look at the mind map for Jasmine's letter and then answer the questions.

Day & Date: Friday, April 1st

To: My little sister, Herry

From: Your older sister, Jasmine

- **little sister's favorite subject:** Music
- **Jasmine's favorite subject:** Art
  - **What to study:** things like painting, drawing and designing
  - **What to bring / what for:** a pencil, a sketchbook, an eraser design a dress

1. Who is the sender of the letter? Who is the receiver?

2. What is Jasmine's favorite subject?

3. What does Jasmine study in art class?

4. What does she need to bring to class?

5. What will she do with them?

Complete Jasmine's letter using the mind map.

6 Writing Practice II

Fill in the mind map by writing information about your letter in the boxes below.

Day & Date: ____________________

To: ____________________ From: ____________________

- Your friend's favorite subject:
- Your favorite subject:
  - What to study:
  - What to bring / what for:

Write your letter using the information you wrote in the mind map.

UNIT 8

E-Mail

1 Reading for Ideas

Read Maria's e-mail and then answer the questions.

To: Ellen@friendly.com
From: Maria@friendly.com
Re: Vacation at an Island

Dear Ellen,

Summer vacation is coming. What are you going to do for vacation?

Every year my family goes on a vacation together. This year we are going to Jeju Island in Korea. It is famous for its beautiful natural scenery, peaceful beaches, Olle tour and delicious food. There are many wonderful sights to see. Manjang Cave, Yeomiji Botanical Garden, and Hallasan National Park are some of them. We will visit them all. We will also do many fun activities at the beach. We are going to ride a banana boat, enjoy water skiing, and make sand castles. We will try Korean foods such as Kimchi, Kalbi, and Bibimbap. I am so excited about going. I cannot wait it!

Please tell me about your vacation plans too. I look forward to hearing from you soon about what you'll be doing.

Bye.

Sincerely,
Maria

1. What does Maria's family do every summer vacation?
2. Where is her family going on a vacation this summer?
3. Why does her family decide to go there?
4. What activities will her family do there?
5. What Korean food will her family try?

2 Focusing on Grammar

Look at the examples below and then make the sentences similar to the examples.

1. will + 동사원형
   ➡ 1) 이미 결정된 것이 아니고 말하는 순간에 하겠다고 결정하는 경우
   2) 무언가를 하겠다고 제안할 때
   3) 무언가를 하겠다고 동의할 때
   4) 무언가를 하겠다고 약속할 때
   5) 누군가에게 무언가를 해달라고 부탁할 때
   6) 주로 probably, I expect, I'm sure, I (don't) think, I wonder와 함께

- Did you call him?
  ➡ Oh, no, I totally forgot. I'll do it now.

  ____.

- That bag looks heavy. I'll help you.

  ____.

- Can you give me this book?
  ➡ Sure, I'll give it to you.

  ____.

- I won't tell anyone what you said. I promise.

  ____.

- It's hot. Will you open the door?

  ____.

2. be going to + 동사원형

➡ 1) 이미 결정되어 있거나, ~할 의향이 있는 일을 표현하고자 할 때

2) 주어진 상황에 의하여 미래에 생길 수 있는 일을 표현하고자 할 때

- Are you going to watch the movie on TV tonight?
  ➡ No, I'm going to go to bed early.
- What is she going to do with that money?
  ➡ She's going to buy a new car.
- I'm just going to make a quick call. Can you wait for me?

____.

____.

- Look at the clouds in the sky! It's going to rain.
- I feel bad. I think I'm going to be sick.

____.

____.

3. will + 동사원형 / be going to + 동사원형 비교

- Mary phoned while you were out.
  ➡ OK. I'll call her back.
  ➡ Yes, I know. I'm going to call her back.

- Let's have a party(Mary is talking to Suzan).
  ➡ That's a good idea. We'll invite many friends.

- Suzan and I have decided to have a party (Mary meets Helen.).
  ➡ We're going to invite a lot of people.

- Look at those black clouds in the sky.
  ➡ It's going to rain. (not "It will rain.")

- I feel terrible. I think I'm going to be sick. (not "I think I'll be sick.")

- Mary will probably get here at about 5 o'clock. (not "Mary is going to get here at about 5 o'clock.")

- These shoes are very well-made. They'll last a lcng time. (not "They are going to last a long time.")

- I think the weather will be nice this afternoon. (= I think the weather is going to be nice this afternoon.)

4. look forward to + 명사 / 동명사
   ➡ '명사 / 동명사'를 기대하다

- This semester he is looking forward to getting a scholarship.
- My sister is looking forward to getting a raise this year.

____.

____.

3 Learning Sentence Structures

Write the sentences in English using the words in the parentheses.

1. 메리와 톰은 다음 달에 결혼할 예정이다. (get married)

2. 내가 이 카메라의 사용법을 알려주겠다. (how to use)

3. 비가 온다. 우산 없이 나가면 옷이 젖을 거야. (get wet)

4. 추워요. 창문 좀 닫아 주시겠습니까? (It is cold)

5. 목이 말라요. 마실 것 좀 주시겠습니까? (I'm thirsty)

6. 나는 너를 곧 만나기를 기대하고 있다. (look forward to)

7. 그는 살 집을 찾고 있다. (a house to live in)

8. 많은 사람들이 크리스마스를 기대하고 있다. (look forward to)

4 Common Mistakes

Correct the thirteen mistakes and then rewrite the paragraph.

To : Sook@friendly.com
From : Young@friendly.com
Re : Vacation in London

Dear Suk,

My family go on a vacation every year. This year we is going to goes to the London during summer vacation. it is a active and exciting city at england. The 2012 Summer Olympics will is hold there from July 28th to August 13th. We will visit several stadium to watch games. London is famous two-story buses and trams. It is also famous for musicals. We will watching musicals in the theater. How cool the vacation will be!

Bye.

Sincerely,
Young

5 Writing Practice I

Look at the mind map for Maria's e-mail and then answer the questions.

1. Where is Maria going on a vacation this summer?

2. Why does she choose the place for vacation?

3. What will Maria do there?

4. What is the place famous for?

Write an e-mail based on the mind map.

To :
From :
Re :

6 Writing Practice II

Fill in the mind map by writing information about your email in the boxes below.

Write an e–mail using the information you wrote in the mind map.

To :
From :
Subject :

UNIT 9

Having a Pet

1 Reading for Ideas

Read 'Having a Pet' and then answer the questions.

Having a Pet

Many people like animals and keep a dog or a cat as a pet. My sister and I want to get a squirrel as a pet. It is very exciting to have a squirrel as a pet. It cannot bark like a dog, but it can climb trees. It can run on a wheel, too. We can play with it all the time, but it cannot go into the market with us. We will take good care of our pet by feeding it hard food such as nuts. We will bathe and groom it. We will take it to the vet when it is sick. Keeping a squirrel as a pet will not be easy, but it will be a lot of fun. What a wonderful friend it will be!

1. What kind of animal do they want to have as a pet?

2. What can a squirrel do?

3. Where will they go when it is sick?

4. What kind of food does it like?

5. Do you have any pets? If so, what pet do you have?

2 Focusing on Grammar

Look at the examples below and then make the sentences similar to the examples.

1. It ~ to부정사
   ➡ 가주어 'It', 진주어 'to부정사'

- It is almost impossible to master English in a month.
- It is important to help students find their aptitude in middle school and high school.

____.

____.

2. it ~ to부정사
   ➡ 가목적어 'it', 진목적어 'to부정사'

- Many supporters made it difficult for him to speak.
- What made it difficult for you to go there?

____.

____.

3. It ~ that 주어+동사
   ➡ 가주어 'It', 진주어 'that 이하'

- It is almost impossible that we'll master English in a month.

- It is important that we help students find their aptitude in middle school and high school.

____.

____.

4. It ~ for(of)목적격 + to부정사
   ➡ 가주어 'It', 의미상의 주어 'for(of)목적격', 진주어 'to부정사'

- It is not right for her to say that she is innocent of any of the allegations.
- It is foolish of you to do that.

____.

____.

5. When 주어 + 동사, 주어 + 동사 = 주어 + 동사 when 주어 + 동사
   ➡ ~할 때, ~하다

- When it rains, I usually stay home.
  ➡ I usually stay home when it rains.
- When you finish the project, you should check it again.

____.

____.

6. should + 동사원형
   ➡ ~하는 게 좋겠다 (충고)

- If you are sick, you shouldn't go to school.
- The government should do more to reduce suicide.

______________________________.

______________________________.

7. must(have to) + 동사원형
   ➡ ~해야 한다 (강요)

- You must wear a uniform when you go to school.
- Be quite. You mustn't make any noise.

______________________________.

______________________________.

8. 동명사(동사원형 + -ing)
   ➡ 주어, 보어, 목적어 역할

- Playing the piano is a good way to reduce stress.
- My hobby is listening to music.
- I am considering going to Canada to study English.

______________________________.

______________________________.

3 Learning Sentence Structures

Write the sentences in English using the words in the parentheses.

1. 교통체증이므로 대중교통을 이용하는 것이 좋겠다. (heavy traffic)

2. 너 누구에게도 그것을 말하면 안 된다. (anyone else)

3. 어린이들이 컴퓨터게임을 오래 하는 것은 좋지 않다. (games)

4. 내가 아줌마 집에 방문했을 때 그녀는 통화를 하고 있었다. (talk on the phone)

5. 그녀는 시간이 있을 때 수영하는 것을 즐긴다. (her free time)

6. 벽에 사진을 거는 것이 좋겠다. (put ~ on)

7. 실수를 하는 것이 영어를 배우는 방법이다. (make mistakes)

8. 이 책은 우리가 영작을 쉽게 할 수 있도록 해준다. (make sentences)

4 Common Mistakes

Correct the twenty mistakes and then rewrite the paragraph.

Most the people like an animal and have a dog or a cat as a pet. I regret that I don't like some animals, even a dog or a cat. Probable you will think it is impersonal. When I am in high school, a dog with a white tail and long fur lived on my house. The dog was love by my family. One day on the summer, when it was really hot, I slept with the door opening, and I heard a strange sound. I opened my eye and saw the dog sit in front the door. When I saw a dog, I uttered a shriek of terror. As soon as I uttered, the dog run up to me. After that day, I was horrify by every animals. When I meet a dog in the street, I am afraid to passing by it. This is why I don't like any animal.

5 Writing Practice I

Look at Tom's mind map and then answer the questions.

Keeping a dog as a pet

INTRODUCTION

- **What kind:** a dog
- **Wanted looks:** gray-and white fur & dark eyes

BODY

- **Things it can do:** fetch a ball, take a walk with me, play with me
- **Things it can't do:** go to a restaurant with the family
- **How to take care:** feed, bathe, cut nails of it, take it to the vet when sick

CLOSING

- **How I feel:** hard, but great

1. What kind of pet does Tom want to have?

2. What things can the pet do?

3. What will Tom do when his pet is sick?

4. How does Tom feel about having a pet?

Write Tom's essay using the mind map.

6 Writing Practice II

Fill in the mind map by writing information about your essay in the boxes below.

TITLE: ______________________

INTRODUCTION	BODY	CLOSING

Write your own essay using the information you wrote in the mind map.

UNIT 10 Shopping for Groceries

1 Reading for Ideas

Read 'Groceries Shopping for Mom' and then answer the questions.

Groceries Shopping for Mom

My mother's birthday was last Wednesday. I wanted to cook a special meal for her with my sister. My sister and I decided to make pizza. We needed to buy ingredients to make it. Before we went to the grocery store, we made a shopping list. We wrote down mushrooms, tomatoes, a can of olives, a bottle of pickles, shrimp, bell peppers, onions, and cheese. At the grocery store, we put those things in the shopping cart. The woman at the store helped us pick up the things on the shopping list. After we had all the things in our cart, we went to check out. The cashier at the counter was very kind. After that I bagged all our groceries. We came home and made pizza. My mom said the pizza was so good. We were very happy.

1. What did she and her sister want to make for their mom?

2. What did they do before they went to the grocery store?

3. What did they get at the grocery store?

4. Who helped them at the grocery store? How?

5. What did their mom say about the pizza?

2 Focusing on Grammar

Look at the examples below and then make the sentences similar to the examples.

1. Before 주어+동사, 주어+동사=주어+동사 before 주어+동사
   ➡ ~하기 전에 ~하다

- Before she has a meal, she washes her hands.
- She washes her hands before she has a meal.

____.

____.

2. Before 명사/동명사
   ➡ ~하기 전에

- Before meals, wash your hands.
- Wash your hands before eating.

____.

____.

3. After 주어+동사, 주어+동사=주어+동사 after 주어+동사
   ➡ ~ 후에 ~ 하다

- After he wrote down some ingredients, he went to the store.
- He went to the store after he wrote down some ingredients.

____.

____.

4. After 명사 / 동명사
➡ ~ 후에

- After writing down some ingredients, he went to the store.
- After meals, brush your teeth.

____.

____.

5. decide + 목적어(명사)
➡ '명사'를 결정하다

- The court decided the case against the plaintiff.

____.

6. decide + 목적어(to부정사) :
➡ 'to부정사' 하기로 결정하다

- I decided to have a sandwich and a cup of coffee for my lunch.
- We decided not to go out because it was cold.

____.

____.

7. decide that 주어+동사
➡ '주어'가 '동사' 하기를 결심하다

- She decided that she would become a lawyer at the age of 10.
- The government decided that they will give the singer an order of cultural merit.

____.

____.

8. say that 주어+동사
➡ '주어'가 '동사' 하다고 말하다

- He says that she is not guilty.
- She said that he didn't want to discuss it right now.

____.

____.

3 Learning Sentence Structures

Write the sentences in English using the words in the parentheses.

1. 요리하기 전에 손을 씻는 것을 잊지 마라. (don't forget)

2. 식사 후 즉시 설거지를 해주세요. (wash the dishes)

3. 집에 도착하자마자 생선을 냉장고에 넣는 것이 좋겠다. (put ~ in)

4. 우리 부모님은 형을 만나기 위해 미국에 가기로 결정했다. (decided to)

5. 우리 부모님은 그들이 형을 만나러 미국에 갈 거라고 나에게 말했다.

6. 그녀는 내년에 결혼할 것이라고 말한다. (get married)

7. 나는 엄마를 위해 맛있는 팬케이크를 만들기로 결정했다. (tasty pancakes)

8. 그는 감자 껍질을 벗긴 후 삶았다. (peel, steam)

4 Common Mistakes

Correct the fifteen mistakes and then rewrite the paragraph.

My brother birthday was last Saturday. He like fried dumplings and I decided to make it for him. First, I went to grocery store to buy some ingredient. I bought a cabbage, meats, onions, and so on. after I bought it, I go to the counter to pay. When I come home, I started to make dumplings by myself. It took me about 2 hour to make it. He ate them and said he love them very much. Making dumplings were not easy. It was a long day.

5 Writing Practice I

Look at July's mind map and then answer the questions.

Groceries Shopping

- What event:
  my father's birthday
- How you felt:
  good → great
- How you shopped:
  went with my sister
  put the things in the shopping cart
  went to the counter and paid put them in the shopping bag
- What food:
  curry and rice
- What you did first:
  made a shopping list
- What's on the list:
  pork, potatoes, onions carrots, and curry seasoning

1. What did she want to make for her father?

2. What did she do first?

3. What did she get at the grocery store?

4. Who went with her to the grocery store?

Write July's essay based on the mind map.

6 Writing Practice II

Fill in the mind map by writing information about your own groceries shopping in the boxes below.

Groceries Shopping

- What event:
- How you felt:
- How you shopped:
- What food:
- What you did first:
- What's on the list:

Write about your groceries shopping using the information you wrote in the mind map.

UNIT 11

Invitation

1 Reading for Ideas

Read the invitation and then answer the questions.

Join Our Party!

Please come to our performers' club party!
There will be plenty of food and beverages.
There will be singing, dancing, and acting.
Come and enjoy the party!
We will have a great time.
When: Friday, October 17th
4 p.m.~6 p.m.
Where: City Community Center
on 23 Maple Street
Come with your friends.
Please let us know by October 15th
if you will come.
For more information, call Anny (008-321-2456).

1. What kind of party is it?
2. When and where will the party be held?
3. What should you bring to the party?
4. What should you do if you want to join the party?
5. What should you do if you want more information about the party?

2 Focusing on Grammar

Look at the example below and then make the sentences similar to the examples.

1. 동사원형 + 목적어(명사)
   ➡ ~하라(명령문)

- In order to make a cup of coffee, first boil the water.
- Second, put a teaspoon of coffee in a cup.
- Third, pour the boiling water into the cup.
- Fourth, add milk and / or sugar according to taste.
- And finally, stir the coffee.

____.

____.

2. Don't 동사원형 + 목적어(명사)
   ➡ ~하지마라(부정명령문)

- Don't talk during class.
- Don't cross the road when the traffic light is red.

____.

____.

3. Could you, Would you, Can you, Will you + 동사원형
   Do you think you could + 동사원형 ~ ?
   ➡ 상대방에게 무언가를 부탁할 때

- Could (can) you wait a moment, please?
- Would (will) you please be quiet? I'm thinking about the project.
- Do you think you could lend me this book until next week?

____.

____.

____.

4. 사역동사(make, have, let) + 목적어(명사) + 목적보어(원형부정사)
   ➡ '명사'가 '원형부정사'하게 하다

- She won't let anyone enter the room.
- I made the two lines parallel.
- When did you last have your hair cut?

____.

____.

____.

5. 사역동사(make, have, let) + 목적어(명사) + 목적보어(과거분사)
➡ '명사'가 '과거분사' 되도록 하다

- He had the letter typed.
- It is difficult to make myself understood in English.

____.

____.

____.

3 Learning Sentence Structures

Write the sentences in English using the words in the parentheses.

1. 나는 그에게 그의 차를 청소하도록 했다. (let)

2. 어제 엄마는 집근처 미장원에서 파마를 했다. (perm, a beauty salon)

3. 돈 좀 빌려 주시겠습니까? (lend)

4. 추우니 문을 열지 마세요. (It is cold)

5. 가장 가까운 은행이 어디인지 알려 주시겠습니까? (Could you~)

6. 그 뉴스가 나의 아빠를 슬프게 했다. (make)

7. 술을 마셨으면 운전하지 마라. (drunk)

8. 눈이 충혈됐다. 눈검사를 해야겠다. (bloodshot, examine)

4 Common Mistakes

Correct the ten mistakes and then rewrite the paragraph.

Ms. Kim and Mr. Lee, together with parents, are please to invite you their wedding ceremony. The ceremony is at 2:00 p.m. Sunday, October 12th at the Pleasantville Community Church in 24 Maple Street. We have reserve a party room at the hotel at 5 o'clock for the reception. Please respond as soon as possible – if there is fewer than thirty guest who are attend the reception, we will cancelled the party room.

5 Writing Practice I

Look at the mind map for the invitation and then answer the questions.

It's Party Time

- **What kind of party:** Halloween
- **Preparations:** food, drinks snacks & music

- **When:** Friday, October 31th 4 p.m. ~ 7 p.m.
- **Where:** My office on Main Street

- **For the party:** Costumes–pirates, witches come with your friends

- **Name:** Ann
- **Phone number:** 008–133–4658

1. What kind of party is it?

2. What will be at the party?

3. Who will have the party?

4. When and where is the party?

5. What should invited people wear that day?

Write an invitation using the mind map from the previous page.

6 Writing Practice II

Fill in the mind map by writing information about an invitation in the boxes below.

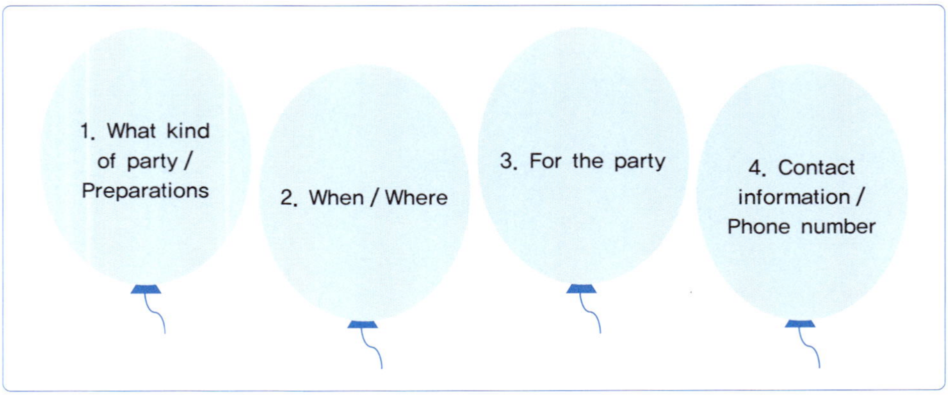

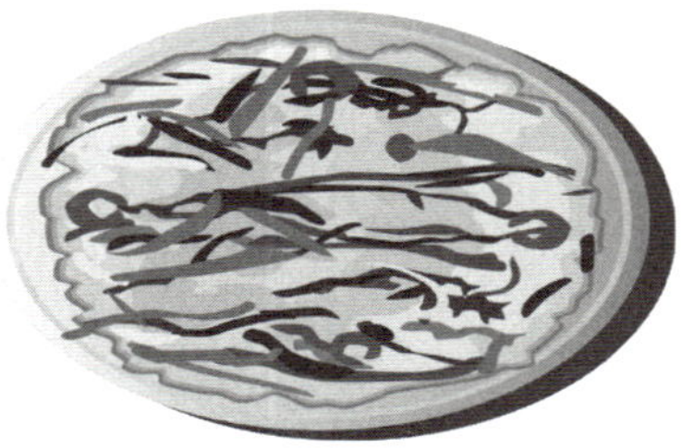

Write about an invitation using the information you wrote in the mind map.

UNIT 12 Poster

1 Reading for Ideas

Read the poster and then answer the questions.

Dog Missing

Please help me find my adorable dog, Mary.
She was last seen running through the park on 23th Maple street.
She is about seven months old.
She is a small white poodle with black eyes.
She has a short tail and large paws.
She weighs about eight pounds and is about one and a half feet long.
She is wearing a red and black collar with an ID tag on it.
She is very friendly around people and loves children.
I am offering a 100 dollar reward for finding Mary.
Please contact me at 324-5784 if you find her.

1. Who is Mary?

2. What should you do if you find the missing puppy?

3. What does Mary look like?

4. What color is the collar that Mary is wearing?

5. Where was she seen last?

2 Focusing on Grammar

Look at the examples below and then make the sentences similar to the examples.

1. 지각동사

see, hear, watch, feel + 목적어(명사) + 목적보어(원형부정사 / 현재분사)

➡ '명사'가 '원형부정사 / 현재분사'를 보고, 듣고, 느끼다

- I heard them discuss(discussing) the price at the store.
- He is watching entertainers perform(performing) on TV.
- We listened to musicians sing(singing) or play(playing) instruments on the stage.
- Everywhere we see people laboring, some of them morning, noon, and night.

______________________________.

______________________________.

______________________________.

2. 지각동사(see, hear, feel) + 목적어(명사) + 목적보어(과거분사)

➡ '명사'가 '과거분사'되는 것을 보고, 듣고, 느끼다

- I saw the building in front of my house burnt down.
- She felt herself lifted up.

______________________________.

______________________________.

______________________________.

3. 능동태 ➡ 주어가 행위를 하는 것
수동태 ➡ 주어가 무언가에 의해서 행위되어지는 것

- The company employs two hundred people.
  ➡ Two hundred people are employed by the company.
- He built the house in 1960.
  ➡ The house was built in 1960 by him.

____.

____.

____.

____.

- The man on the street gave the police the information.
  ➡ The police were given the information by the man on the street.
  ➡ The information was given to the police by the man on the street.
- I sent my friends several e-mails this afternoon.
  ➡ My friends were sent several e-mails this afternoon.(×)
  ➡ Several e-mails were sent to my friends this afternoon.

____.

____.

____.

____.

- I saw the bird singing on the tree.
  - ➡ The bird was seen singing on the street.

____.

____.

- I heard them say(saying) goodbye to their friends.
  - ➡ They were heard to say(saying) goodbye to their friends.

____.

____.

3 Learning Sentence Structures

Write the sentences in English using the words in the parentheses.

1. 나는 1980년 서울에서 태어났다.

2. 나는 길 건너편에서 내 이름이 불리는 것을 들었다. (across the street)

3. 그의 형은 매일 그에게 영어를 가르쳐 준다. (teach)

4. 그는 매일 형에게 영어 가르침을 받는다.

5. 얼마나 많은 사람이 그 사고로 다쳤니? (injure, in the accident)

6. 다친 다섯 명이 병원으로 실려 갔습니다. (take ~ to)

7. 그 정부정책은 시민들의 지지를 받지 못하고 있다. (support)

8. 나는 아르바이트를 하고 시간당 6,000원을 받는다. (a part time job, per hour)

4 Common Mistakes

Correct the thirteen mistakes and then rewrite the paragraph.

May I have you attention, please? We have lost little girl at the information center. She is about 6 year old, and she name is Mary. She has a long blond hair with big eye. She is wearing blue jean and a red and a yellow shirt. She say that she came here with her parent and her young brother. Will the parent of Mary please come to the information center as soon as possible? She is waiting to you.

5 Writing Practice I

Look at the mind map for the poster and then answer the questions.

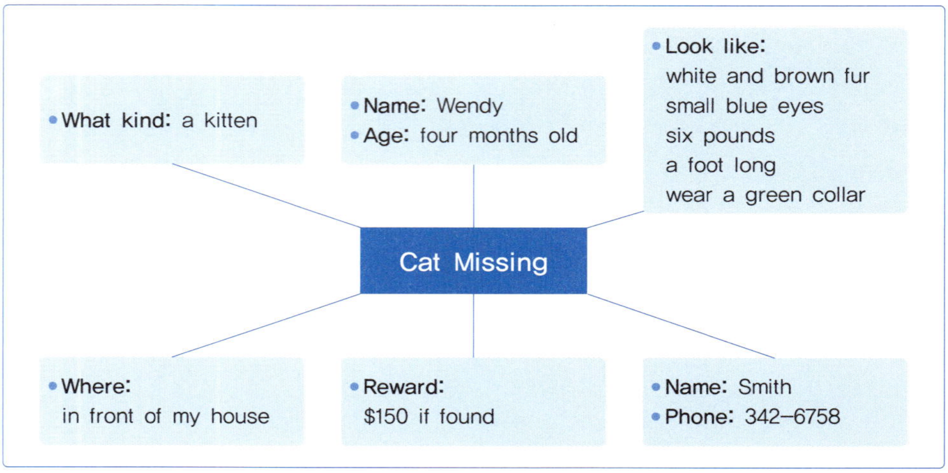

1. What kind of pet is Smith looking for?

2. What's her name and how old is she?

3. What does she look like?

4. Where was she last seen?

5. Is there any reward available?

Create a poster using the mind map from the previous page.

6 Writing Practice II

Fill in the mind map by writing information about a poster in the boxes below.

Missing a Pet

- What kind:

- Name:
- Age:

- Look like:

- Where:
- When:

- Reward:

- Name:
- Phone:

Make your own poster using the information you wrote in the mind map.

First Step for Writing

Answer Key

Unit 1 About Me

1 Reading for Ideas

1. Where does she come from?
   ➡ She comes from Malaysia
2. What's she majoring in?
   ➡ She is majoring in linguistics and English literature.
3. What does she like to do?
   ➡ She likes to read books, especially sci-fi novels.
4. What does she look like?
   ➡ She is short and a little bit overweight. She has short curly black hair with small black eyes.
5. What do you like to do in your free time?
   ➡ I like listening to music in my free time.

3 Learning Sentence Structures

Write the sentences in English using the words in the parentheses.

1. 그는 일본 도쿄에 살고 있다. (Tokyo, Japan)
   He lives in Tokyo, Japan.
2. 나는 책을 읽으면서 음악을 듣는 것을 좋아한다. (listen to)
   I like to listen(listening) to music and read(reading) books.
3. Mary는 대학 졸업 후 은행원이 되고 싶어 한다. (after graduating)
   Mary wants to be a banker after graduating.

4. 우리 학교의 영어선생님은 40대이다. (in his 40s)

The English teacher in my school is in his 40s.

5. 그의 엄마는 앞으로 그가 선생님이 되기를 원한다. (to be a teacher)

His mother wants him to be a teacher in the future.

6. 한국의 부모님들은 사교육에 많은 돈을 소비한다. (private education)

The parents in Korea spend too much money on private education.

7. 한국인들은 영어 공부하는데 너무 많은 돈과 시간을 소비한다.

Koreans spend too much money and time studying English.

8. 그녀는 혼자 밤에 컴퓨터게임 하는 것을 좋아한다. (play computer games)

She likes to play(playing) computer games alone at night.

4 Common Mistakes

Correct the twelve mistakes and then rewrite the paragraph.

my(My) name is Lee, Soonhee. I am from Korea. I am majoring at(in) child development at an(a) university in the U.S. I am a university junior. after(After) graduating, i(I) want to teach kids at a kindergarten in Korea. I lives(live) with my sister's family here. I am a(x) short and slim. Also, I have short curly hair with big black eye(eyes). I am a(x) kind of (an) introverted person. I like to staying(stay) home and read comic books. I like my classmates. They is(are) very kind and friendly.

5 Writing Practice I

1. What's the girl's name?

   ➡ Her name is Younghee.

2. How old is she?

   ➡ She is in her early 20s.

3. How many sisters or brothers does she have ?

   ➡ She has one sister.

4. What is she studying and why?

   ➡ She is studying physics because she wants to be a scientist.

5. What does she like to do in her free time?

   ➡ She likes to fold paper and draw pictures.

Unit 2 My Friend

1 Reading for Ideas

1. Who is Pablo?

➡ He is from Spain and a junior at Madrid University.

2. What is he like?

➡ He is energetic and outgoing. He always smiles and likes to help people.

3. What does he look like?

➡ He is not short and not tall, either. He has short blond hair with big blue eyes.

4. What's his major?

➡ His major is statistics.

5. What does he like doing?

➡ He likes taking pictures.

3 Learning Sentence Structures

Write the sentences in English using the words in the parentheses.

1. 그는 사과도 좋아하고 오렌지도 역시 좋아한다. (too)

He likes apples and oranges, too.

2. 요즈음 나는 좀처럼 학교에 결석하지 않는다. (seldom)

These days, I am seldom late for school.

3. 내 동생은 일찍 일어나지도 않고 학교에 일찍 가지도 않는다. (either)

My sister doesn't get up early and doesn't go to school, either.

4. 우리 아빠는 종종 친구와 직장이 끝난 후 테니스를 한다. (after work)

My father often plays tennis with his friend after work.

5. 내 친구는 부모님에게 항상 매우 친절하고 공손하다. (be polite to)

My friend is always kind and polite to his parents.

6. 우리 오빠는 수학은 잘하지만 영어는 못한다. (good, poor)

My brother is good at mathematics, but he is poor at English.

7. 내 친구와 나는 음악시간에 종종 바이올린을 함께 연주한다.

My friend and I often play the violin together in music class.

8. 나는 일요일에 때때로 여자 친구와 영화를 보러 간다. (go to the movies)

I sometimes go to the movies with my girlfriend on Sunday.

4 Common Mistakes

Correct the fifteen mistakes and then rewrite the paragraph.

Let me introduce my friend to you. His name is Youngjae. He is at(in) his early 20s. He is (a) sophomore in(at) Eulji University at(in) Seongnam. He live(lives) near Seongnam. He is not talls(tall), but he is handsome. He has shortly(short) straight black hairs(hair) with black eye(eyes). He is brave but(and) humorous. He like(likes) read(to read, reading) comic books. He always tell(tells) jokes to his friends, so he has many friend(friends) around his(him).

5 Writing Practice I

1. What's the name of Amon's friend?

   ➡ His name is Bonjang.

2. What is he majoring in at the university?

   ➡ He is majoring in engineering at the university.

3. What does he look like?

   ➡ He is tall and good-looking.

4. What kind of person is he?

   ➡ He is friendly, patient, and responsible. He is also a hard worker.

5. What does he like to do in his free time?

   ➡ He likes to play computer games and play tennis.

Unit 3 My Family

1 Reading for Ideas

1. How many people are there in Suzan's family?
   ➡ There are four people in her family.
2. What does her father do?
   ➡ He is a teacher at a high school.
3. What does her father like to do?
   ➡ He likes cooking at home.
4. What does her mother look like?
   ➡ She is short, but beautiful and smart.
5. What is her sister's favorite subject?
   ➡ She likes mathematics.

3 Learning Sentence Structures

Write the sentences in English using the words in the parentheses.

1. 하루에 커피를 몇 잔 마십니까? (How much coffee ~)
   How much coffee do you drink a day?
2. 너는 너의 방을 청소하는데 얼마나 걸리니? (How long ~)
   How long does it take to clean your room?
3. 그의 방 가운데에 소파와 의자가 있습니다. (There are)
   There are chairs and a sofa in the middle of the room.

4. 밖에 나가서 십분 동안 휴식을 합시다. (a 10 minute break).

Let's go out and take a 10 minute break.

5. 그는 매주 일요일 엄마가 세탁하는 것을 돕습니다. (the laundry)

He helps her mother with the laundry every Sunday.

6. 그는 뇌물을 받아서 10년형을 받았다. (take bribes, a 10 year jail term)

Because of taking bribes he was sentenced to a 10 year jail term.

7. 빨간색을 선호하십니까? 오렌지색을 선호하십니까? (prefer)

Do you prefer red or orange?

8. 내 가방에는 책도 공책도 없습니다. (in my backpack)

There are not any books and notebooks in my backpack.

4 Common Mistakes

Correct the fifteen mistakes and then rewrite the paragraph.

Here is Robert's family's photo. there(There) is(are) four member (members) in the family. their(Their) names are Mr. and Mrs. Baroni, Bruno and Roberto. Mr. Baroni is sit(sitting) on the bed. A night table is beside the bed and window(a window) is between a dresser and a night table. There are(is) a rug on the floor. Mr. Baroni work(works) in the factory. Mrs. Baroni work(works) in a(an) office and always use(uses) a computer. Bruno play(plays) the violin with a bow. roberto(Roberto) likes to play the(x) baseball. When he plays baseball, he wears a helmet and an(a) uniform. He is a good pitcher.

5 Writing Practice I

1. How many people are there in Smith's family?

   ➡ There are four people in his family.

2. What does Smith's mother like to do?

   ➡ She likes to cook and take care of her garden.

3. Where does his sister go?

   ➡ She goes to high school.

4. What does Smith's father do?

   ➡ He is a writer.

Unit 4 My Day

1 Reading for Ideas

1. What did Elias do after he got up?
   ➡ She took a shower, got dressed, ate breakfast, brushed her teeth, and put on some makeup.

2. How did she get to school?
   ➡ She went to school by subway.

3. What did she do in her first class?
   ➡ She learned about writing, wrote a funny story and told it to her classmates.

4. What did she do after school?
   ➡ She went to work.

5. When did she come back from work?
   ➡ She came back from work around 10 p.m.

3 Learning Sentence Structures

Write the sentences in English using the words in the parentheses.

1. 나는 매일 5시부터 8시까지 도서관에서 일한다. (from ~ to)
   I work at the library from 5 p.m. to 8 p.m. everyday.

2. 그는 자주 모든 사람에게 재미있는 이야기를 한다. (funny stories)
   He often tells funny stories to everyone.

3. 그녀는 어젯밤에 10시경에 잠자리에 들었다. (go to bed)
   She went to bed at about 10 p.m. last night.

4. 나는 밤에 음악을 듣고 책을 읽는다. (at night)

I listen to music and read books at night.

5. 그는 술을 너무 많이 마셔서 똑바로 걸을 수가 없었다. (drink alcohol, walk straight)

He couldn't walk straight because he drank too much alcohol.

6. 허리가 아파서 병원에 갔다. (backache)

I went to see a doctor because of a backache.

7. 우리 부서는 한 달에 2번 회의를 한다. (twice a month)

Our department has meetings twice a month.

8. 그는 어젯밤 9시에 나에게 전화했다. (last night)

He called me at 9 p.m. last night.

4 Common Mistakes

Correct the eighteen mistakes and then rewrite the paragraph.

i(I) got up this morning at 8:00. I was late, so I quickly wash(washed) my face. I drink(drank) a glass of milk and brush(brushed) my teeth. And then I feed(fed) my pet. I take(took) a bus and arrived at school at 8:50 a.m. It takes about 30 minutes to get to school by bus. My first class was japanese(Japanese). I learn(learned) about the Japanese alphabet. I did a good job in class and enjoy(enjoyed) it. After class I meet(met) one of my friend(friends) and go(went) to see a movie. Around 10:00 p.m. I come(came) back home. My mother is(was) little(a little) angry because I am(was) late. I was so tire(tired), but I do(did) my homework.

5 Writing Practice I

1. What did John do at 6:30?

   ➡ He got up at 6:30.

2. What did John do at school?

   ➡ He took a test and had lunch.

3. What did John do at 8 p.m.?

   ➡ He went home at 8 p.m.

4. What did John do at the library?

   ➡ He prepared for exams.

5. When did John go to bed?

   ➡ He went to bed at midnight.

Unit 5 My Favorite Sports

1 Reading for Ideas

1. What sport does Anderson like to play?

   ➡ He likes to play tennis.

2. What season is good for the sport? Why?

   ➡ Fall is a good season to play tennis because it is not so hot and not so cold.

3. Who taught him how to play tennis?

   ➡ His uncle taught him how to play tennis.

4. What do you think is the best way to learn something?

   ➡ Practice is the best way to learn something.

5. What is he doing these days?

   ➡ He is teaching how to play tennis to his brother.

3 Learning Sentence Structures

Write the sentences in English using the words in the parentheses.

1. 그는 내년에 승진하길 바란다. (get promoted)

   He hopes that he will get promoted next year.

2. 이맘때 치고는 따뜻하다. (for this time of the year)

   It is warm for this time of the year.

3. 그는 키도 크고 똑똑하고 잘 생겼다고 생각한다. (intelligent)

   I think that he is tall, intelligent and handsome.

4. 어제는 일요일이었다. (Sunday)

It was Sunday.

5. 그것이 완전히 거짓이라고 생각하지 않는다. (false)

I don't think that it is totally false.

6. 여기서 우체국까지는 얼마나 걸릴까요? (the post office)

How long does it take to get to the post office from here?

7. 해외에 가면 나와 엄마는 쇼핑을 즐긴다. (go abroad)

When my mother and I go abroad, we enjoy shopping.

8. 그는 그의 아빠 건강이 곧 회복되길 바란다. (get well soon)

He hopes that his father will get well soon.

4 Common Mistakes

Correct the fourteen mistakes and then rewrite the paragraph.

I likes(like) skiing. Winter is (a) good season for skiing. I learned how to skiing(ski) from my brother-in-law five year(years) ago. It was hard to learning(learn) how to slide down the hill. I fell down many time(times) in the snow, (but) I didn't give up. I practice(practiced) it very hard for a while. Now I enjoy skiing. It is cool. It is excite(exciting) and thrilling, too. I need ski boot(ski boots), ski poles, goggles, (and) ski gloves for skiing. Also I need (a) ski suit for it. I like it because it help(helps) me to be healthy. I hope winter come(comes) soon.

5 Writing Practice I

1. What sport do you like to play?

   ➡ I like to play badminton.

2. What season is good for the sport?

   ➡ Spring is good for the sport.

3. Who taught you how to play badminton?

   ➡ My father taught me how to play badminton.

4. What equipment do you need to play badminton?

   ➡ I need a racket and a shuttlecock.

5. What are you hoping to do in the future?

   ➡ I hope that I become a good player in the future.

Unit 6 My Dream Job

1 Reading for Ideas

1. What does Paul want to be?

   ➡ He wants to be a chef.

2. Who is Paul's role model?

   ➡ It is his mother.

3. What did his mom do at home?

   ➡ She made lots of wonderful food and baked delicious cookies and bread for her family.

4. How did he feel when he helped his mom cook?

   ➡ He was so happy.

5. What should he do to be a chef?

   ➡ He studies and practices a lot.

3 Learning Sentence Structures

Write the sentences in English using the words in the parentheses.

1. 이 책은 내가 영문법을 공부하는데 도움이 될 것이다. (English grammar)

   This book will help me study English grammar.

2. 그가 들어올 수 있도록 그에게 열쇠를 주었다. (come in)

   I gave him the key so that he could come in.

3. 슬픈 소식이 나를 울렸다. (The sad news)

   The sad news made me cry.

4. 이리 와서 설거지 좀 도와주세요. (wash the dishes)

Please come and help me with washing the dishes.

5. 어제 오후에 나는 내 동생에게 연을 만들어주었다. (a kite)

I made my brother a kite yesterday afternoon.

6. 우리는 같은 문제를 반복하지 않기 위해서 협력해야 한다. (cooperate)

We have to cooperate so as not to repeat the same problem.

7. 지난 일요일 아빠가 우리를 위해서 빵과 과자를 만들었다. (bread)

Last Sunday, my father baked some bread and cookies for us.

8. 햇볕이 강해서 얼굴에 선크림을 발랐다. (wear sunscreen)

It was really sunny and I wore sunscreen on my face.

4 Common Mistakes

Correct the thirteen mistakes and then rewrite the paragraph.

I am interested in make(making) people beautiful. After graduating, i(I) want to be a hairdresser likely(like) Ms. Lee at(in) my town. She run(runs) many shops around the country. She is friend(friendly), pretty, and smart. There is(are) a lot of customers in her shop all the time. Three year(years) ago I met and told to(x) her that I wanted to be a hairdresser somedays(someday). She encouraged me and told me many things about be(being) a hairdresser. I know that it isn't an(x) easy to be a hair dresser like her. I should to(x) try to practice more, and I will.

5 Writing Practice 1

1. What do you want to do after graduating?

   ➡ I want to be a doctor.

2. Why did you want to be a doctor?

   ➡ My mother was sick and was in the hospital for a month.

3. What should you do to be a doctor?

   ➡ I should study biology hard.

4. What will you do as a doctor?

   ➡ I will help sick people like my mom.

5. Who is your role model?

   ➡ It is the doctor who took care of my mom.

Unit 7 Letter

1 Reading for Ideas

1. Who wrote the letter?
   ➡ Mary wrote the letter.
2. Who did Mary write it to?
   ➡ Mary wrote it to Wendy.
3. What class does Mary like the most? How about Wendy?
   ➡ Mary likes English the most. Wendy's favorite subject is biology.
4. What should Mary bring to class tomorrow?
   ➡ Mary should bring an English-Spanish dictionary to class tomorrow.
5. What will Mary do during English class tomorrow?
   ➡ Mary will study how to write an essay and write her essay.

3 Learning Sentence Structures

Write the sentences in English using the words in the parentheses.

1. 당황해서 어떻게 해야 할지 몰랐다. (at a loss)
   I was at a loss so I didn't know what to do.
2. 모든 사람이 그가 시험에 합격해서 놀랐다. (pass)
   Everyone was surprised when he passed the exam.
3. 나는 그녀가 그 과제를 빨리 끝내주었으면 좋겠다. (the project)
   I need her to finish the project early.

4. 영화가 실망스러워서 우리는 실망했다. (disappoint)

The movie was so disappointing that we were disappointed.

5. 나는 지난 주말에 5시간 영어공부를 하였다. (last weekend)

I studied English for 5 hours last weekend.

6. 지난 겨울방학에 영어공부 하러 미국에 갔었다. (last winter vacation)

I went to America to study English last winter vacation.

7. 그는 책을 읽는 동안에 재미있는 무언가를 배웠다. (something interesting)

While he was reading the book, he learned something interesting.

8. 수업 중에 친구로부터 문자를 받았다. (text messages)

I got several text messages from my friend during class.

4 Common Mistakes

Correct the sixteen mistakes and then rewrite the paragraph.

May 10th, Monday

Dear Jeongsuk,

How have you been do(doing)? I am fine. It is (a) really sunny day today. All kinds of flowers is(are) blooming. I'm sitting in(on) the grass. There is(are) many students around I(me). Some are talking with their friends and other(others) are reading and relaxing(relaxed). It is a beautiful scene, isn't it? I'm happy to hearing(hear) that you are coming to California visiting(to visit) me. It's not too hot and not too cold, too(either). I have five class(classes): composition, grammar, vocabulary, speaking, and reading every weeks(week). I have three classes a day and study twenty-four hour(hours) a week. After class, I enjoy to talk(talking) with my classmates from other country(countries). They are mostly from Asia. I hope I can meet you as soon as possible.

Take care

Sincerely,

Yoon

5 Writing Practice I

1. Who is the sender of the letter? Who is the receiver?

   ➡ Jasmine sent the letter. Her sister received it.

2. What is Jasmine's favorite subject?

   ➡ It is art.

3. What does Jasmine study in art class?

   ➡ She studies painting, drawing and designing.

4. What does she need to bring to class?

   ➡ She needs to bring a pencil, a sketchbook, and an eraser.

5. What will she do with them?

   ➡ She will design a dress.

Unit 8 E-Mail

1 Reading for Ideas

1. What does Maria's family do every summer vacation?
   ➡ Her family goes on a vacation together every summer.

2. Where is her family going on a vacation this summer?
   ➡ Her family is going to Korea's Jeju Island this summer.

3. Why does her family decide to go there?
   ➡ It is famous for beautiful natural scenery, peaceful beaches, Olle tour and delicious food.

4. What activities will her family do there?
   ➡ Her family is going to ride a banana boat, enjoy water skiing, and make sand castles.

5. What Korean food will her family try?
   ➡ Her family will try Kimchi, Kalbi, and Bibimbop.

3 Learning Sentence Structures

Write the sentences in English using the words in the parentheses.

1. 메리와 톰은 다음 달에 결혼할 예정이다. (get married)
   Mary and Tom are going to get married next month.

2. 내가 이 카메라의 사용법을 알려 주겠다. (how to use)
   I will show you how to use the camera.

3. 비가 온다. 우산 없이 나가면 옷이 젖을 거야. (get wet)
   It is raining. You are going to get wet when you go out without an umbrella.

4. 추워요. 창문 좀 닫아 주시겠습니까? (It is cold)

It is cold. Would you please close the window?

5. 목이 말라요. 마실 것 좀 주시겠습니까? (I'm thirsty)

I'm thirsty. Would you give me something to drink?

6. 나는 너를 곧 만나기를 기대하고 있다. (look forward to)

I am looking forward to seeing you.

7. 그는 살 집을 찾고 있다. (a house to live in)

He is looking for a house to live in.

8. 많은 사람들이 크리스마스를 기대하고 있다. (look forward to)

Many people are looking forward to Christmas.

4 Common Mistakes

Correct the thirteen mistakes and then rewrite the paragraph.

To : Sook@friendly.com
From : Young@friendly.com
Re : Vacation in London

Dear Suk,

My family go(goes) on a vacation every year. This year we is(are) going to goes(go) to the(x) London during summer vacation. it(It) is a(an) active and exciting city at(in) england(England). The 2012 Summer Olympics will is(be) hold(held) there from July 28th to August 13th. We will visit several stadium(stadiums) to watch games. London is famous (for) two-story buses and trams. It is also famous for musicals. We will watching(watch) musicals in the theater. How cool the vacation will be!

Bye.

Sincerely,
Young

5 Writing Practice I

1. Where is Maria going on a vacation this summer?

   ➡ She is going to France this summer.

2. Why does she choose the place for vacation?

   ➡ Because it is a lovely and beautiful place.

3. What will Maria do there?

   ➡ She will visit the Eiffel Tower, the Seine River, and the Arc de Triomphe.

4. What is the place famous for?

   ➡ It is famous for wine and perfume.

Unit 9 Having a Pet

1 Reading for Ideas

1. What kind of animal do they want to have as a pet?
   ➡ They want to have a squirrel as a pet.

2. What can a squirrel do?
   ➡ It can climb trees and run on a wheel.

3. Where will they go when it is sick?
   ➡ They will take it to the vet.

4. What kind of food does it like?
   ➡ It likes hard food such as nuts.

5. Do you have any pets? If so, what pet do you have?
   ➡ No, I don't have any.
   ➡ Yes, I have a cat.

3 Learning Sentence Structures

Write the sentences in English using the words in the parentheses.

1. 교통체증이므로 대중교통을 이용하는 것이 좋겠다. (heavy traffic)
   Because of heavy traffic, you should use public transportation.

2. 너 누구에게도 그것을 말하면 안 된다. (anyone else)
   You mustn't tell it to anyone else.

3. 어린이들이 컴퓨터게임을 오래 하는 것은 좋지 않다. (games)
   It is not good for children to play computer games for a long time.

4. 내가 아줌마 집에 방문했을 때 그녀는 통화를 하고 있었다. (talk on the phone)

When I visited my aunt's house, she was talking on the phone.

5. 그녀는 시간이 있을 때 수영하는 것을 즐긴다. (her free time)

She enjoys swimming in her free time.

6. 벽에 사진을 거는 것이 좋겠다. (put ~ on)

You should put the picture on the wall.

7. 실수를 하는 것이 영어를 배우는 방법이다. (make mistakes)

Making mistakes is a way to learn English.

8. 이 책은 우리가 영작을 쉽게 할 수 있도록 해준다. (make sentences)

This book helps us make sentences in English easily.

4 Common Mistakes

Correct the twenty mistakes and then rewrite the paragraph.

Most the people(people) like an(x) animal(animals) and have a dog or a cat as a pet. I regret that I don't like some(any) animals, even dogs or cats. Probable(Probably) you will think it is impersonal. When I am(was) in high school, a dog with a white tail and long fur lived on(in) my house. The dog was love(loved) by my family. One day on(in) the summer, when it was really hot, I slept with the door opening(open), and I heard a strange sound. I opened my eye(eyes) and saw the dog sit(sitting) in front (of) the door. When I saw a(the) dog, I uttered a shriek of terror. As soon as I uttered it, the dog run(ran) up to me. After that day, I was horrify(horrified) by every animals(animal). When I meet a dog in(on) the street, I am afraid to passing(pass) by it. This is why I don't like any animal(animals).

5 Writing Practice I

1. What kind of pet does Tom want to have?

   ➡ He wants to have a dog.

2. What things can the pet do?

   ➡ The dog can fetch a ball, take a walk with him, and play with him.

3. What will Tom do when his pet is sick?

   ➡ He will take it to the vet.

4. How does Tom feel about having a pet?

   ➡ He feels tired, but great.

Unit 10 Shopping for Groceries

1 Reading for Ideas

1. What did she and her sister want to make for their mom?
   ➡ They wanted to make pizza for their mom.

2. What did they do before they went to the grocery store?
   ➡ They made a shopping list before they went to the grocery store.

3. What did they get at the grocery store?
   ➡ They bought mushrooms, tomatoes, a can of olives, a bottle of pickles, shrimp, bell peppers, onions, and cheese.

4. Who helped them at the grocery store? How?
   ➡ The woman at the store helped them pick up the things on the shopping list.

5. What did their mom say about the pizza?
   ➡ Their mom said that the pizza was so good.

3 Learning Sentence Structures

Write the sentences in English using the words in the parentheses.

1. 요리하기 전에 손을 씻는 것을 잊지 마라. (don't forget)
   Don't forget to wash your hands before cooking.

2. 식사 후 즉시 설거지를 해 주세요. (wash the dishes)
   Wash the dishes right away after meals.

3. 집에 도착하자마자 생선을 냉장고에 넣는 것이 좋겠다. (put ~ in)
   You should put the fish in the refrigerator as soon as you get home.

4. 우리 부모님은 형을 만나기 위해 미국에 가기로 결정했다. (decided to)

Our parents decided to go to America to see my brother.

5. 우리 부모님은 그들이 형을 만나러 미국에 갈 거라고 나에게 말했다.

Our parents told me that they were going to America to see my brother.

6. 그녀는 내년에 결혼할 것이라고 말한다. (get married)

She says that she is going to get married next year.

7. 나는 엄마를 위해 맛있는 팬케이크를 만들기로 결정했다. (tasty pancakes)

I decided to make tasty pancakes for my mom.

8. 그는 감자 껍질을 벗긴 후 삶았다. (peel, steam)

After he peeled these potatoes, he steamed them.

4 Common Mistakes

Correct the fifteen mistakes and then rewrite the paragraph.

My brother(brother's) birthday was last Saturday. He like(likes) fried dumplings and I decided to make it(them) for him. First, I went to (the) grocery store to buy some ingredient(ingredients). I bought a cabbage, meats(some meat), onions, and so on. after(After) I bought it(them), I go(went) to the counter to pay. When I come(came) home, I started to make (the) dumplings by myself. It took me about 2 hour(hours) to make it(them). He ate them and said he love(loved) them very much. Making dumplings were(was) not easy. It was a long day.

5 Writing Practice I

1. What did she want to make for her father?

   ➡ She wanted to make curry and rice for her father.

2. What did she do first?

   ➡ She made a shopping list first.

3. What did she get at the grocery store?

   ➡ She got pork, potatoes, onions, carrots, and curry seasoning.

4. Who went with her to the grocery store?

   ➡ She went to the grocery store with her sister.

Unit 11 Invitation

1 Reading for Ideas

1. What kind of party is it?

➡ It is the performers' club party.

2. When and Where will the party be held?

➡ The party will be held on Friday, October 17th from 4 p.m to 6 p.m at the City Community Center on 23 Maple Street.

3. What should you bring to the party?

➡ I can bring my friends to the party.

4. What should you do if you want to join the party?

➡ I let them know by October 15th.

5. What should you do if you want more information about the party?

➡ I can call Anny at 008-321-2456.

3 Learning Sentence Structures

Write the sentences in English using the words in the parentheses.

1. 나는 그에게 그의 차를 청소하게 시켰다. (let)

I let him clean his car.

2. 어제 엄마는 집 근처 미장원에서 파마를 했다. (perm, a beauty salon)

My mom had her hair permed at the beauty salon near my house yesterday.

3. 돈 좀 빌려 주시겠습니까? (lend)

Could you lend me some money?

4. 추우니 문을 열지 마세요. (It is cold)

It is cold. Don't open the door.

5. 가장 가까운 은행이 어디인지 알려 주시겠습니까? (Could you~)

Could you please tell me where the nearest bank is?

6. 그 뉴스가 나의 아빠를 슬프게 했다. (make)

The news made my father sad.

7. 술을 마셨으면 운전하지 마라. (drunk)

Don't drive when you are drunk.

8. 눈이 충혈됐다. 눈검사를 해야겠다. (bloodshot, examine)

I had bloodshot eyes. I should have them examined.

4 Common Mistakes

Correct the ten mistakes and then rewrite the paragraph.

Ms. Kim and Mr. Lee, together with (their) parents, are please(pleased) to invite you (to) their wedding ceremony. The ceremony is at 2:00 p.m. (On) Sunday, October 12th at the Pleasantville Community Church in(on) 24 Maple Street. We have(have to) reserve a party room at the hotel at 5 o'clock for the reception. Please respond as soon as possible – if there is(are) fewer than thirty guest(guests) who are (to) attend the reception, we will cancelled(cancel) the party room.

5 Writing Practice I

1. What kind of party is it?

   ➡ It is a Halloween party.

2. What will be at the party?

   ➡ There will be food, drinks, snacks and music.

3. Who will have the party?

   ➡ Ann will have the party.

4. When and Where is the party?

   ➡ The party will be held on October 31th from 4 p.m to 7 p.m at Ann's office on Main Street.

5. What should invited people wear that day?

   ➡ They should wear costumes: pirates and witches.

Unit 12 Poster

1 Reading for Ideas

1. Who is Mary?

   ➡ Mary is a dog.

2. What should you do if you find the missing puppy?

   ➡ I should call 432-5784.

3. What does Mary look like?

   ➡ She has a short tail and large paws. She also has black eyes.

4. What color is the collar that Mary is wearing?

   ➡ She is wearing a red and black collar.

5. Where was she seen last?

   ➡ She was last seen running through the park on 23th Maple street.

3 Learning Sentence Structures

Write the sentences in English using the words in the parentheses.

1. 나는 1980년 서울에서 태어났다.

   I was born in Seoul in 1980.

2. 나는 길 건너편에서 내 이름이 불리는 것을 들었다. (across the street)

   I heard my name called from across the street.

3. 그의 형은 매일 그에게 영어를 가르쳐 준다. (teach)

   His brother teaches him English every day.

4. 그는 매일 형에게 영어 가르침을 받는다.

He is taught English by his brother every day.

5. 얼마나 많은 사람이 그 사고로 다쳤니? (injure, in the accident)

How many people were injured in the accident?

6. 다친 다섯 명이 병원으로 실려 갔습니다. (take ~ to)

Five injured people were taken to the hospital.

7. 그 정부정책은 시민들의 지지를 받지 못하고 있다. (support)

The government's policy was not supported by citizens.

8. 나는 아르바이트를 하고 시간당 6,000원을 받는다. (a part time job, per hour)

I have a part time job and I am paid 6000 won per hour.

4 Common Mistakes

Correct the thirteen mistakes and then rewrite the paragraph.

May I have you(your) attention, please? We have (a) lost little girl at the information center. She is about 6 year(years) old, and she(her) name is Mary. She has a(x) long blond hair with big eye(eyes). She is wearing blue jean(jeans) and a red and a(x) yellow shirt. She say(says) that she came here with her parent (parents) and her young(younger) brother. Will the parent(parents) of Mary please come to the information center as soon as possible? She is waiting to(for) you.

5 Writing Practice I

1. What kind of pet is Smith looking for?

   ➡ He is looking for a kitten.

2. What's her name and how old is she?

   ➡ It is Wendy and she is four months old.

3. What does she look like?

   ➡ She has white and brown fur and small blue eyes.

4. Where was she last seen?

   ➡ She was last seen in front of my house.

5. Is there any reward available?

   ➡ There is a $150 reward.

References

Anne Taylor, Garrett Byrne. (2007). *Very Easy Toeic*. Seoul: Compass Publishing.

Christopher Thompson. (2007). *Access Toeic*. Seoul: Moonjin Media Co, Ltd.

Raymond Murphy. (2007). *English Grammar in Use*. KHL Printing Co Pte Ltd.

The Korea Times. (2012). www. Koreatimes.co.kr.

Writing Star Basic. (2010). Young & Son Global, Inc. Printed and distributed in Korea by YBM.

Writing Star I. (2010). Young & Son Global, Inc. Printed and distributed in Korea by YBM.

저자약력

성명희(Myeong-Hee Seong)

Ph.D., Korea University

신윤희(Yoon-Hee Shin)

MA, California State University, Fullerton

First Step for Writing

2012년 12월 26일 초판 1쇄 인쇄
2012년 12월 28일 초판 1쇄 발행

저 자 성 명 희 · 신 윤 희
발행인 寅製 진 욱 상
발행처 백산출판사

저자와의 합의하에 인지첩부 생략

서울시 성북구 정릉3동 653-40
등록 : 1974. 1. 9. 제 1-72호
전화 : 914-1621, 917-6240
FAX : 912-4438
http://www.ibaeksan.kr
editbsp@naver.com

값 14,000원
ISBN 978-89-6183-661-6